Science Biographies

Charles
Darwin

Nick Hunter

Raintree is an imprint of Capstone Global Library Limited, a company incorporated in England and Wales having its registered office at 7 Pilgrim Street, London, EC4V 6LB – Registered company number: 6695582

www.raintreepublishers.co.uk
myorders@raintreepublishers.co.uk

Text © Capstone Global Library Limited 2014
First published in hardback in 2014
The moral rights of the proprietor have been asserted.

Edited by Dan Nunn, Adam Miller, and Diyan Leake
Designed by Cynthia Akiyoshi
Original illustrations © Capstone Global Library Ltd 2014
Picture research by Hannah Taylor and Tracy Cummins
Production by Helen McCreath
Originated by Capstone Global Library
Printed and bound in China

ISBN 978 1 406 27245 1
17 16 15 14
10 9 8 7 6 5 4 3 2

Hunter, Nick
Darwin, Charles. (Science biographies)
A full catalogue record for this book is available from the British Library.

Acknowledgements
We would like to thank the following for permission to reproduce photographs: akg-images p. 10; Alamy Images pp. 4 (© North Wind Picture Archives), 19 (© Mark Phillips), 24 (© Mary Evans Picture Library); Bridgeman Art Library pp. 7 (© English Heritage Photo Library), 16 (© English Heritage Photo Library); Corbis pp. 14 (Tui De Roy / Minden Pictures), 17 (William Perlman), 25 (PoodlesRock), 26 (EPA / Andy Rain), 27 (Bettmann), 28 (Philippe Lissac / Godong); Getty Images pp. 5 (Science & Society Picture Library), 8 (Universal History Archive); Photo Researchers p. 13 (Science Source); Photoshot p. 20 (© UPPA); Science Photo Library pp. 6 (Paul D. Stewart), 18 (SPL), 21 (Paul D. Stewart); Shutterstock pp. 12 (© JaySi), 22 (© Matt Gibson), design elements (© EcOasis, © Tatiana53, © YKh, © leospek, © Matt Ragen); Superstock p. 23 (Universal Images Group); Jim Thies p. 9 (© Jim Thies); Topham Picturepoint p. 15.

Cover photographs of a portrait of Charles Darwin in 1854 and a sketch of a shingled iguana by Charles Darwin reproduced with permission of Bridgeman Art Library.

Contents

Some words are shown in **bold**, like this. You can find out what they mean by looking in the glossary.

Who was Charles Darwin?

Charles Darwin spent his life studying and understanding nature. Darwin's ideas changed the way people understood the natural world. He also changed the way people thought about themselves and where human beings came from.

Charles Darwin grew up at a time when most people believed that God had created the world and everything in it in six days. Darwin studied the world's animals and plants on a five-year voyage around the world. What he discovered convinced him that there must be another explanation for the huge variety of animals and plants on Earth.

This is a portrait of Charles Darwin aged about 45, just before he published his famous theory of **evolution**.

CHALLENGING IDEAS

Darwin's ideas challenged what most people believed at the time. Opponents argued that he was wrong. Some of these arguments continue more than 150 years after Darwin **published** his **theory**. However, scientists accept that Darwin's theories are correct. This makes him one of history's greatest scientists.

Darwin collected samples and drawings of the animals he saw on his travels, such as this rhea from South America.

Growing up

Charles Darwin was born on 12 February 1809 in Shrewsbury, Shropshire. His father was a well-known doctor, and the family was wealthy. Charles grew up in a large house close to the River Severn. When Charles was eight years old, his mother died. His three elder sisters then looked after him.

During his seven years at Shrewsbury School, Charles learned little about science and nature.

School struggles

At the age of nine, Charles was sent to Shrewsbury School. He hated it. Schools at the time thought that learning Latin and ancient Greek was much more important than science. Charles himself later wrote that "nothing could have been worse for the development of my mind".

Charles's terrible school reports did not please his father, who accused him of caring for "nothing but shooting, dogs, and rat-catching". He predicted that his son would be "a disgrace" to Charles himself and all his family.

Charles and his sister Catherine were the youngest of the six Darwin children.

Birds and beetles

Charles was fascinated by nature. He explored the grounds of his family home, collecting beetles and other **specimens**. He also experimented with chemicals in a shed. His smelly experiments earned Charles the nickname "Gas".

The young naturalist

Despairing of Charles's bad results at school, his father sent him to Edinburgh University in Scotland to study medicine. His medical studies were not a success, but the young nature-lover threw himself into scientific research and discussions. Charles explored and collected marine, or sea, animals from the coast close to Edinburgh.

Charles was just 16 years old when he left home to study at Edinburgh University.

Medical misery

Charles soon decided that he would not follow his father into medicine. At the time, patients were operated on without **anaesthetic**. The pain must have been terrible, and Charles was horrified by it. He also found his teachers incredibly boring.

Studying at Cambridge

Charles's father agreed that medicine was not the best career for his son. Charles's next stop was Cambridge University where he would study to join the church. If he became a country **parson**, Charles would have plenty of time to keep collecting beetles and looking under rocks.

Cambridge also gave Charles the chance to meet and learn from some of the world's greatest scientists. One of them, Professor John Stevens Henslowe, suggested to Charles the journey that would change his life and the history of science.

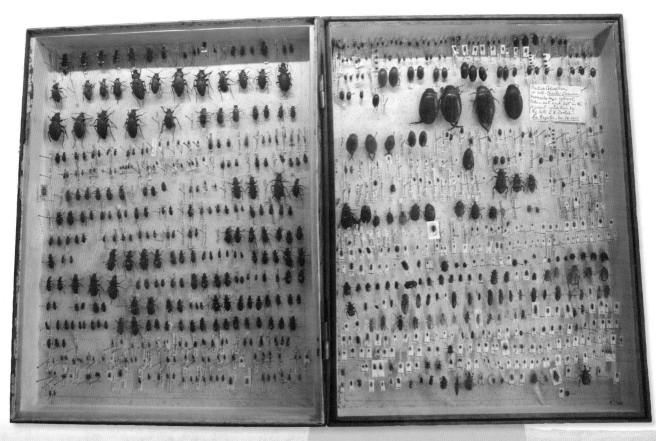

Some specimens have survived from Charles's huge collection of beetles.

The voyage of the Beagle

When HMS *Beagle* sailed from Plymouth on 27 December 1831, Darwin must have been filled with a mixture of excitement and nerves. He had joined the voyage as a **naturalist** and companion for the ship's captain, Robert Fitzroy. Darwin was not used to travelling by sea and was very seasick at the start of the voyage.

Darwin was amazed when he saw how small the *Beagle* was. He had to share his cabin with others on the journey.

The *Beagle* would sail along the coast of South America and travel right around the world before returning to Britain. The journey was planned to last two years, but it actually took more than twice as long. Darwin was free to leave the ship and study the animals and plants he found at any of the ship's many stops.

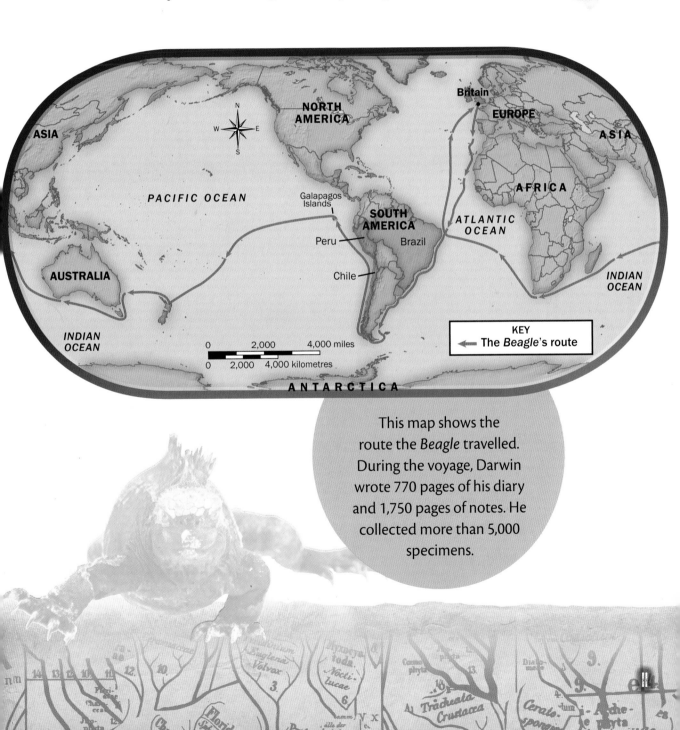

This map shows the route the *Beagle* travelled. During the voyage, Darwin wrote 770 pages of his diary and 1,750 pages of notes. He collected more than 5,000 specimens.

Asking questions

Darwin was constantly asking himself questions about the world around him. In February 1832, the *Beagle* reached the coast of Brazil. Darwin was able to explore the region's **tropical rainforests**. Elsewhere, he discovered **fossils** of large animals such as giant sloths. Darwin wondered what the link was between the fossils he found and the animals that were still living in the rainforests.

Tropical rainforests are home to a greater variety of plants and animals than anywhere else on Earth.

SHOCKING SLAVERY

Darwin's "intense delight" at the living things he found did not include the way human beings treated each other. He was shocked and angered by the **slavery** he saw in Brazil.

As the voyage continued, Darwin saw some astonishing natural forces. He saw a volcanic eruption and experienced an earthquake in Chile.

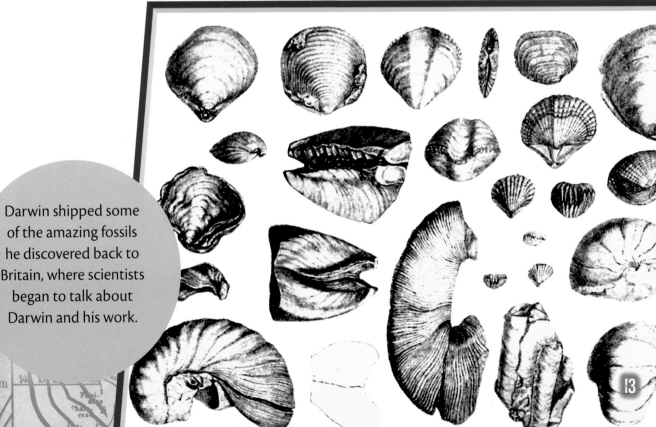

Darwin shipped some of the amazing fossils he discovered back to Britain, where scientists began to talk about Darwin and his work.

The Galapagos Islands

The highlight of Darwin's voyage was his visit to the Galapagos Islands in 1835. The isolated islands lie 1,000 kilometres (about 620 miles) from the coast of South America. Here, Darwin found many **species** that could not be seen anywhere else. He was intrigued by the fact that they were similar to, but slightly different from, species he had found on the mainland.

Charles described the Galapagos as "a little world within itself".

The *Beagle* visited several different islands of the Galapagos. They were just a few kilometres apart but each contained slightly different species of birds and animals, such as the famous giant tortoises. It was only when he returned home that Darwin began to examine the many specimens he had collected.

The giant tortoises of the Galapagos were so big that Darwin and others were able to ride on their backs.

Classifying life

Living things have always been arranged or classified in different groups. For example, cats are a distinct species of animal as they share the same features and can produce **offspring** together. Before Darwin, scientists believed that all species had been created together.

Making sense of life

When Darwin returned home in October 1836, his family hardly recognized him. It is no surprise that he looked different, but Darwin was also different in other ways. The carefree young man returned as a serious scientist who threw himself into his work.

By 1840, Darwin was living in London. He was now a leading member of scientific groups such as the Geological Society and the Royal Society.

BIOLOGY BEST-SELLER

Darwin discovered that his name was now widely known because of the specimens and letters he had sent from the voyage. When he published his journal and notes in 1839, the story of his adventures became a best-selling book.

Darwin set about organizing and studying the specimens he had collected. By 1840, he had worked out most of his theory of evolution. However, it was a long time before he would publish his ideas. Darwin knew that his theory would shake the worlds of science and religion.

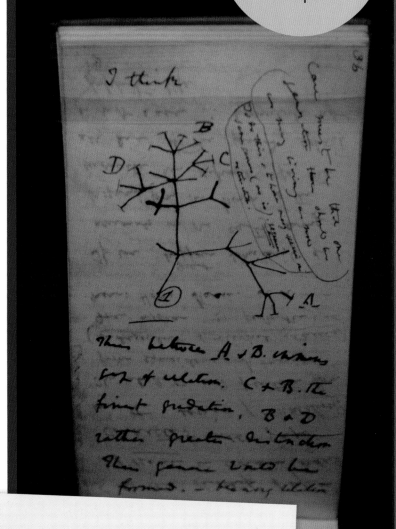

A page from Darwin's notebook shows his ideas taking shape.

Everyday experts

Darwin talked to learned scientists, but also farmers and animal breeders. He even joined a pigeon-fanciers' club to discover more about how people could **breed** animals to pass on different features to their offspring.

Country life

In 1839, Darwin's notes included a list of reasons why he should or should not get married. Although he noted that wives could be a "terrible loss of time", he decided to marry his cousin Emma Wedgwood. He was surprised when she agreed! They married in January 1839. Their first son, William, was born at the end of that year.

This portrait of Emma was painted when she was 32, following her marriage to Darwin.

FAMILY AND TRAGEDY

Darwin and Emma had ten children in total. Large families were common at that time, as lack of medical knowledge meant that children often did not live to become adults. Two of the Darwins' children died as babies. The greatest loss of Darwin's life was the death of his oldest daughter Annie from **typhoid** in 1851.

In 1842, Darwin moved his growing family to Down House in Kent. He lived there for the rest of his life.

Health problems

From about 1840, Darwin was hit by ill health that would stay with him for more than 40 years. He was constantly exhausted and always in pain. His illness meant that Darwin hardly ever left his home.

Publishing the theory

Darwin knew he would have to prove himself if people were going to pay attention to his ideas. He spent eight years working on a study of marine animals called barnacles. This work may not have been as important as evolution, but people now knew that Darwin was an expert naturalist.

GREAT MINDS THINK ALIKE

In 1858, as Darwin worked on his ideas about evolution, he received a letter from another naturalist, Alfred Russel Wallace. In the letter, Wallace set out his own theory, which was the same as Darwin's. Darwin's friends suggested that he should publish some of his own work on evolution at the same time as Wallace. Their ideas were jointly made public a few weeks later.

Alfred Russel Wallace (1823–1913)

Wallace came up with his theory of evolution by **natural selection** during his travels in South America and South East Asia. Darwin knew that Wallace deserved to be recognized as the father of evolution just as much as he was.

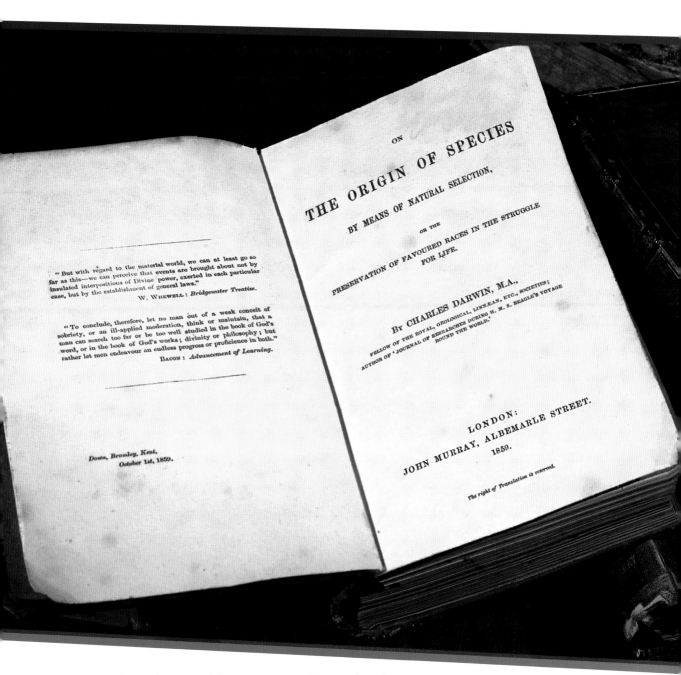

ON

THE ORIGIN OF SPECIES

BY MEANS OF NATURAL SELECTION,

OR THE

PRESERVATION OF FAVOURED RACES IN THE STRUGGLE
FOR LIFE.

By CHARLES DARWIN, M.A.,

FELLOW OF THE ROYAL, GEOLOGICAL, LINNÆAN, ETC., SOCIETIES;
AUTHOR OF ' JOURNAL OF RESEARCHES DURING H. M. S. BEAGLE'S VOYAGE
ROUND THE WORLD.'

LONDON:
JOHN MURRAY, ALBEMARLE STREET.
1859.

The right of Translation is reserved.

"But with regard to the material world, we can at least go so far as this—we can perceive that events are brought about not by insulated interpositions of Divine power, exerted in each particular case, but by the establishment of general laws."

W. WHEWELL: *Bridgewater Treatise.*

"To conclude, therefore, let no man out of a weak conceit of sobriety, or an ill-applied moderation, think or maintain, that a man can search too far or be too well studied in the book of God's word, or in the book of God's works; divinity or philosophy; but rather let men endeavour an endless progress or proficience in both."

BACON: *Advancement of Learning.*

Down, Bromley, Kent,
October 1st, 1859.

Darwin shut himself away and worked on the book that would explain his ideas in full. In November 1859, Darwin's book *On the Origin of Species by Means of Natural Selection* went on sale.

Explaining evolution

Darwin's theory of evolution by natural selection was based on what he had seen and collected on the voyage of the *Beagle*. He had seen that animals usually produce large numbers of offspring. Some of these offspring did not survive to have offspring of their own.

All animals, including humans, are slightly different, even if they share the same parents. Darwin concluded that the ones that survived were the strongest living things, or the ones most suited to their **environment**. They had features that helped them survive and they passed these features on to their offspring.

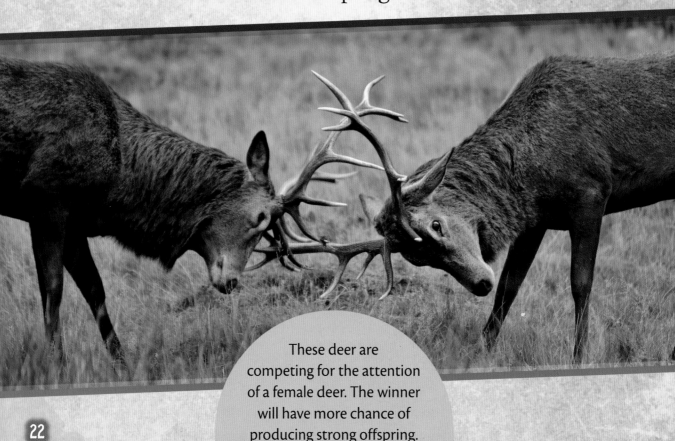

These deer are competing for the attention of a female deer. The winner will have more chance of producing strong offspring.

Living things evolve, or change, over time, because the features of the strongest offspring are passed on. Darwin's theory called this natural selection. The process not only causes species to change but creates new ones. All species are descended from living things that have become **extinct**.

ORNITHOLOGY.

1. Geospiza magnirostris.
2. Geospiza fortis.
3. Geospiza parvula.
4. Certhidea olivacea.

First steps in evolution

The French naturalist Lamarck suggested the first general theory of evolution around the time that Darwin was born. Much of this theory was later proved incorrect, as Lamarck believed living things changed in their lifetimes to suit their environment.

Controversy

Darwin had always known that the theory of evolution would upset some people. Members of the church and many older scientists attacked his ideas. People argued over his theory at public meetings, which Darwin himself was too ill to attend. Younger scientists such as Thomas Henry Huxley spoke instead of him.

BONES AND STONES, AND SUCH-LIKE THINGS.

Thomas Henry Huxley (1825–1895)

Huxley was a **biologist** who had made his name studying marine life on a voyage to Australia. Huxley argued for the theory of evolution in speeches and writings. He earned the nickname "Darwin's bulldog" because of his support for Darwin.

HUMAN ORIGINS

The biggest arguments were over the origins of human beings, although Darwin had been careful not to discuss this tricky subject in his book. Many of Darwin's opponents could not accept that the human species had come about through evolution just like every other living thing. At the time, most people believed that humans were superior to other animals.

Twenty years after Darwin's ideas were published, most scientists agreed that his theory was correct.

A cartoonist pictured Darwin himself as a monkey.

Darwin's last years

Poor health stopped Darwin from leaving Down House, where Emma nursed him. Darwin used the plants and animals around his home to continue his work on evolution. He studied orchids and other flowers in his gardens and greenhouses.

He also explored the origins of humans in his book *The Descent of Man* (1871). His final work in 1881 looked at worms.

Darwin worked in his study at Down House during the later years of his life.

Charles Darwin died on 19 April 1882. He was hugely respected by his friends but also by many people who had attacked his ideas at first. Darwin was buried among Britain's greatest men and women in London's Westminster Abbey.

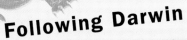

Following Darwin

Before Darwin, biologists could not explain how living things came to exist in the first place. Modern scientists now know how the features of plants and animals are passed on to their offspring. They can even use this knowledge to treat diseases. None of this would be possible without Darwin.

Darwin remained curious and excited by nature even in old age. During his work on worms, he brought them into his house to see if they reacted when Emma played the piano.

In search of Darwin

We know more about Charles Darwin than almost any other scientist. He kept notes and other records of everything he did. He also wrote an account of his own life for his family. Darwin lived before telephones and as he got older he rarely left his house. His discussions with other scientists were written down in more than 15,000 letters. You can even visit Darwin's house and walk along his famous "thinking path".

This statue of Darwin has been at the Natural History Museum in London since 1885.

Timeline

1809 Charles Darwin is born in Shrewsbury, England, on 12 February

1818 Starts to attend Shrewsbury School; dislikes the school and is not a successful student

1825 Begins to study medicine at Edinburgh University

1828 Attends Christ's College, Cambridge; studies to join the church but his interest in nature grows

1831 Leaves Plymouth on HMS *Beagle* on 27 December. The voyage is to shape his ideas and his life.

1835 The *Beagle* visits the Galapagos Islands during September and October. Darwin makes many discoveries that lead to his theory of evolution.

1839 Darwin marries his cousin Emma Wedgwood. The couple's first child, William, is born in December.

1842 The Darwin family moves to Down House in Kent

1844 Darwin sets out his theory of evolution in a long essay, but does not publish his ideas

1858 Receives a letter from Alfred Russel Wallace outlining Wallace's own ideas about evolution. Their ideas are jointly made public.

1859 *On the Origin of Species by Natural Selection* is published, becoming a best-seller

1871 *The Descent of Man* is published, explaining the evolution of human beings

1882 Charles Darwin dies on 19 April at the age of 73

Glossary

adapt change to fit a situation or environment

anaesthetic substance that stops a patient from feeling pain during an operation

biologist someone who studies living things, such as animals and plants

breed produce offspring

environment surroundings in which animals and plants live, including weather, land, and other living things

evolution process by which types of living things develop from earlier forms

extinct no longer alive

fossil remains of an ancient animal or plant, usually found in rock

geologist person who studies the rocks and minerals on and beneath Earth's surface

naturalist person who observes and studies the natural world

natural selection process in which living things that are best adapted to their environment survive and pass on their features to their offspring

offspring young of an animal or plant, such as human children

parson vicar or member of the clergy who works in a church

publish make information or ideas available to people, such as in a printed book

slavery when one person or group of people claims to own and control another person or group

species group of living things that are related to each other and can breed together to produce offspring

specimen one plant or animal used as an example of its type for study

theory series or collection of ideas that are designed to explain something

tropical rainforest type of forest environment found close to the equator that contains the widest variety of animals and plants on Earth

typhoid serious infectious disease which causes the sufferer to have a very high fever

Find out more

BOOKS

Charles Darwin (Lifelines), Alan Gibbons (Kingfisher, 2011)

Charles Darwin and the Beagle Adventure, Amanda Wood (Templar, 2009)

Evolution, Nature, and Stuff, Glenn Murphy (Macmillan/Science Museum, 2010)

Evolution Revolution, Robert Winston (Dorling Kindersley, 2009)

WEBSITES

news.bbc.co.uk/local/kent/hi/people_and_places/history/ newsid_8374000/8374369.stm
This audio slideshow about Charles Darwin's life is narrated by children.

www.nhm.ac.uk/nature-online/science-of-natural-history/ expeditions-collecting/beagle-voyage/index.html
Discover more about the voyage of HMS *Beagle* on this interactive map.

PLACE TO VISIT

Down House
Luxted Road
Downe
Kent BR6 7JT

www.english-heritage.org.uk/daysout/properties/home-of-charles-darwin-down-house

Explore Darwin's home at Down House, Kent.

Index